# FRAMES AND BORDERS VECTOR DESIGNS

# FRAMES AND BORDERS VECTOR DESIGNS

DOVERPICTURA

DOVER PUBLICATIONS, INC. | Mineola, New York

**At Dover Publications we're committed to producing books in an earth-friendly manner and to helping our customers make greener choices.**

Manufacturing books in the United States ensures compliance with strict environmental laws and eliminates the need for international freight shipping, a major contributor to global air pollution. And printing on recycled paper helps minimize our consumption of trees, water and fossil fuels.

The text of this book was printed on paper made with 10% post-consumer waste and the cover was printed on paper made with 10% post-consumer waste. At Dover, we use Environmental Defense's Paper Calculator to measure the benefits of these choices, including: the number of trees saved, gallons of water conserved, as well as air emissions and solid waste eliminated.

Please visit the product page for *Frames and Borders Vector Designs* at www.doverpublications.com to see a detailed account of the environmental savings we've achieved over the life of this book.

By Alan Weller.
Designed by Cristy Goldman and Juliana Trotta.

Copyright © 2011 by Dover Publications, Inc.
Digital images copyright © 2011 by Dover Publications, Inc.
All rights reserved.

*Frames and Borders Vector Designs* is a new work, first published by Dover Publications, Inc., in 2011.

The illustrations contained in this book and CD-ROM belong to the Dover Pictura Electronic Design Series. They are royalty-free, and may be used as a graphic resource provided no more than ten images are included in the same publication or project. The use of any of these images in book, electronic, or any other format for resale or distribution as royalty-free graphics is strictly prohibited.

For permission to use more than ten images, please contact:
Permissions Department
Dover Publications, Inc.
31 East 2nd Street
Mineola, NY 11501
rights@doverpublications.com

The CD-ROM file names correspond to the images in the book. All of the artwork stored on the CD-ROM can be imported directly into a wide range of design and word-processing programs on either Windows or Macintosh platforms. No further installation is necessary.

*ISBN 13: 978-0-486-99123-8*
*ISBN 10: 0-486-99123-7*

Manufactured in the United States of America by Courier Corporation
99123701
www.doverpublications.com

## GALLERY—PAGES 1, 2, 4, 8 thru 25

Provides you with examples, from basic to complex, of compositions designed using vectors and textures from the accompanying CD. On the right-hand side of each pair of pages is an 'asset panel,' in which you will find a listing of all of the components and colors that were used in the creation of the illustrations.

## TUTORIALS—PAGES 26 thru 45

Contains instructional materials pertaining to the examples shown in the Gallery section of this book. Use this section to learn how work with vector images and to create your own compositions in Adobe Illustrator. These tutorials will teach you about basic elements such as shapes, paths, and anchor points, and will give you step-by-step instructions for coloring, reshaping, scaling and patterning.

## BACKGROUND TEXTURES—PAGES 46 and 47

Shows simple, clean renderings of all of the background textures images that are on the accompanying CD.

## VECTORS—PAGES 48 thru 127

Shows simple, clean renderings of all of the vector images that are on the accompanying CD.

# GALLERY

181

028

030

| | |
|---|---|
|  |  |
| BT 022 | BT 020 |
|  |  |
| BT 010 | BT 004 |

**Techniques Used:**
Fill, Gradient, Drop Shadow,
Inner Shadow, Flip, Scale, Stroke

| | 8c | 40m | 57y | 0k |
| | 0c | 31m | 86y | 0k |
| | 38c | 29m | 80y | 0k |

| | 230r | 163g | 117b |
| | 253r | 183g | 62b |
| | 170r | 164g | 89b |

# GALLERY

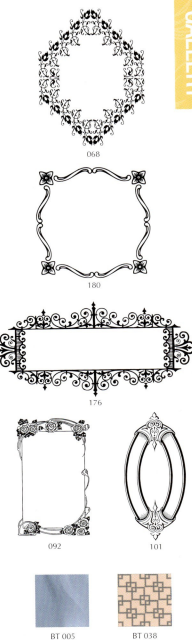

068

180

176

092  101

BT 005  BT 038

**Techniques Used:**
Fill, Drop Shadow,
Clipping Mask, Scale, Rotate

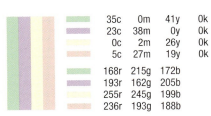

| | 35c | 0m | 41y | 0k |
| | 23c | 38m | 0y | 0k |
| | 0c | 2m | 26y | 0k |
| | 5c | 27m | 19y | 0k |
| | 168r | 215g | 172b | |
| | 193r | 162g | 205b | |
| | 255r | 245g | 199b | |
| | 236r | 193g | 188b | |

116

045

BT 003   BT 006   BT 001

**Techniques Used:**
Fill, Gradient, Drop Shadow,
Clipping Mask, Scale

| | | | | |
|---|---|---|---|---|
| | 79c | 27m | 100y | 13k |
| | 56c | 0m | 56y | 0k |
| | 18c | 0m | 70y | 0k |
| | 21c | 61m | 69y | 0k |
| | 62r | 130g | 62b | |
| | 115r | 196g | 145b | |
| | 216r | 227g | 117b | |
| | 202r | 122g | 91b | |

**GALLERY**

062

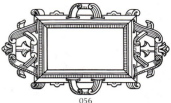
056

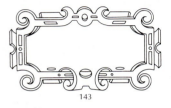
143

035

BT 008

BT 021

BT 011

BT 017

**Techniques Used:**
Fill, Gradient, Drop Shadow, Clipping Mask, Scale, Rotate

| | | | | |
|---|---|---|---|---|
| | 15c | 0m | 20y | 0k |
| | 10c | 22m | 0y | 0k |
| | 3c | 1m | 19y | 0k |
| | 215r | 234g | 211b | |
| | 223r | 200g | 225b | |
| | 247r | 244g | 214b | |

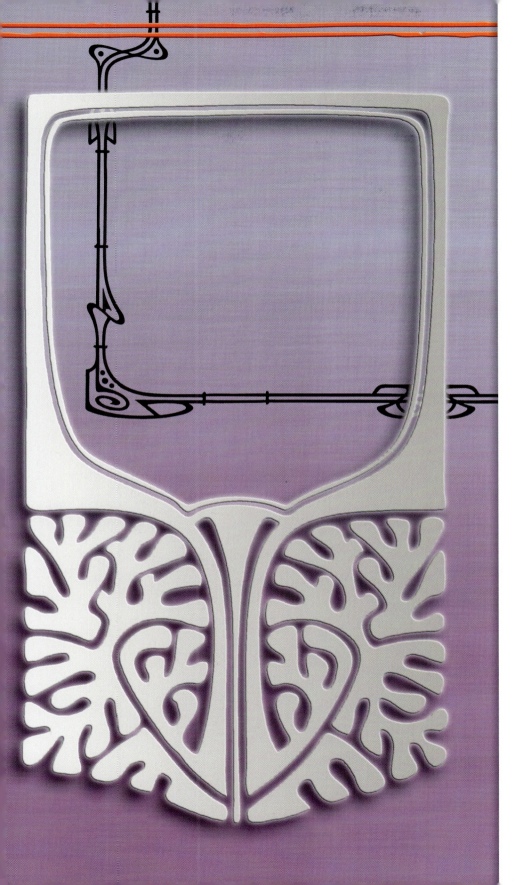

178

177

038  167

122  113

BT 007

**Techniques Used:**
Fill, Gradient, Drop Shadow, Clipping Mask, Scale, Rotate, Bevel/Emboss

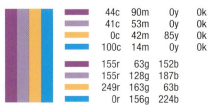

| | | | | |
|---|---|---|---|---|
| | 44c | 90m | 0y | 0k |
| | 41c | 53m | 0y | 0k |
| | 0c | 42m | 85y | 0k |
| | 100c | 14m | 0y | 0k |
| | 155r | 63g | 152b | |
| | 155r | 128g | 187b | |
| | 249r | 163g | 63b | |
| | 0r | 156g | 224b | |

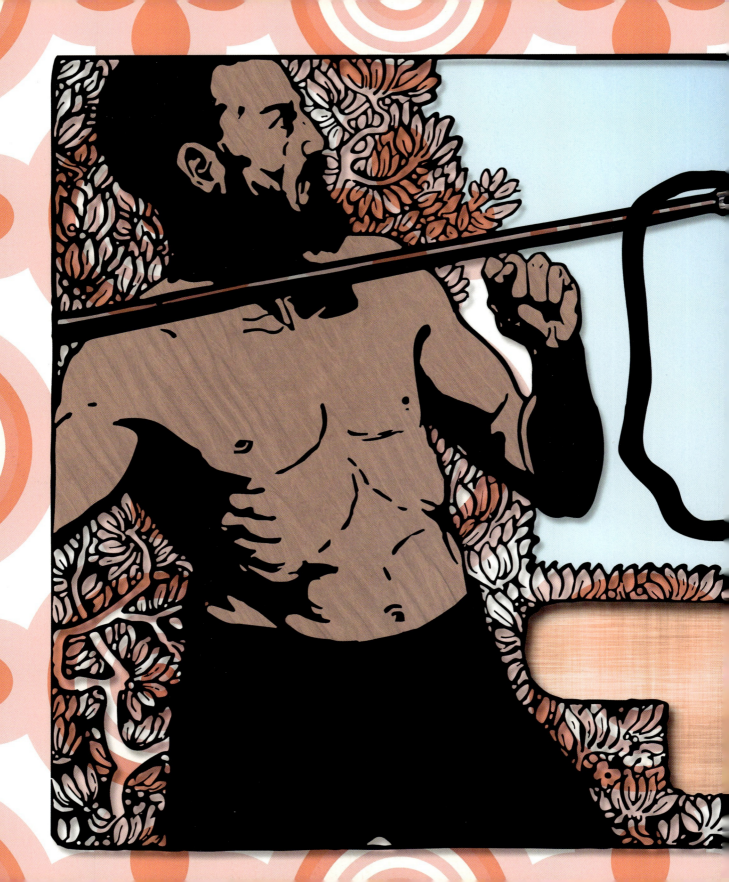

GALLERY

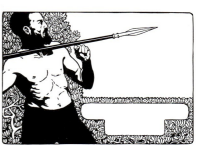

047

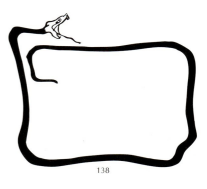

138

BT 037    BT 024    BT 007

**Techniques Used:**
Fill, Gradient, Drop Shadow, Clipping Mask, Scale, Rotate

| | 1c | 60m | 51y | 0k |
| | 49c | 2m | 0y | 0k |
| | 0c | 26m | 11y | 0k |
| | 25c | 48m | 45y | 1k |

| | 227r | 114g | 47b |
| | 115r | 203g | 243b |
| | 250r | 200g | 202b |
| | 191r | 140g | 129b |

19

GALLERY

003

208

057

SP 001

SP 002

BT 014

BT 023

BT 017

**Techniques Used:**
Fill, Gradient, Clipping Mask, Scale, Rotate, Bevel/Emboss

| | 56c | 48m | 47y | 13k |
| | 31c | 36m | 44y | 1k |
| | 28c | 22m | 48y | 0k |
| | 23c | 19m | 18y | 0k |
| | 115r | 115g | 115b | |
| | 177r | 154g | 139b | |
| | 188r | 183g | 144b | |
| | 195r | 194g | 196b | |

21

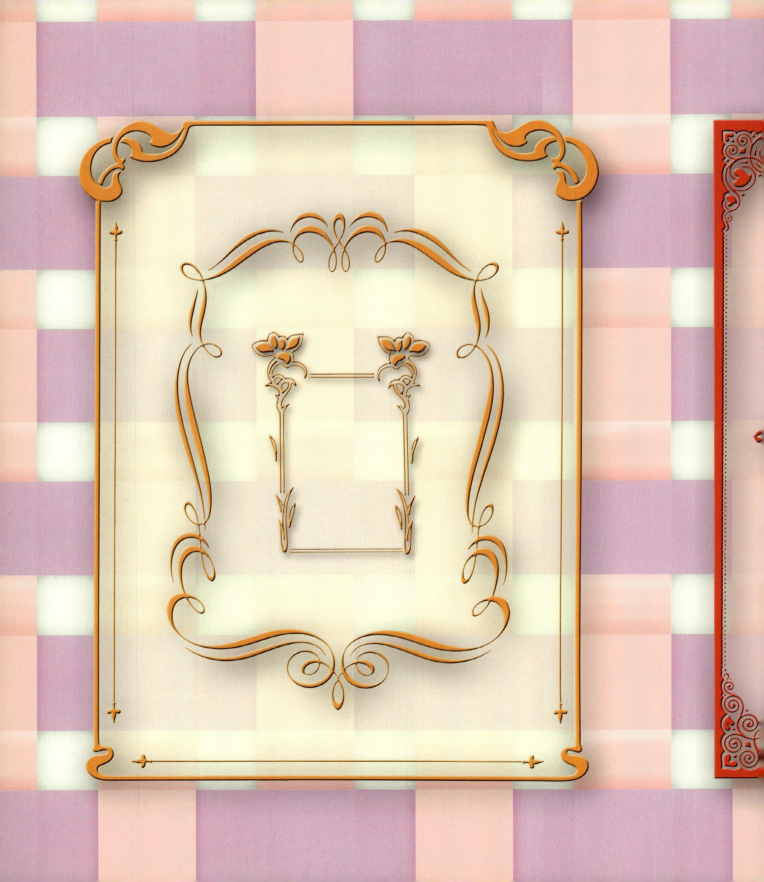

# GALLERY

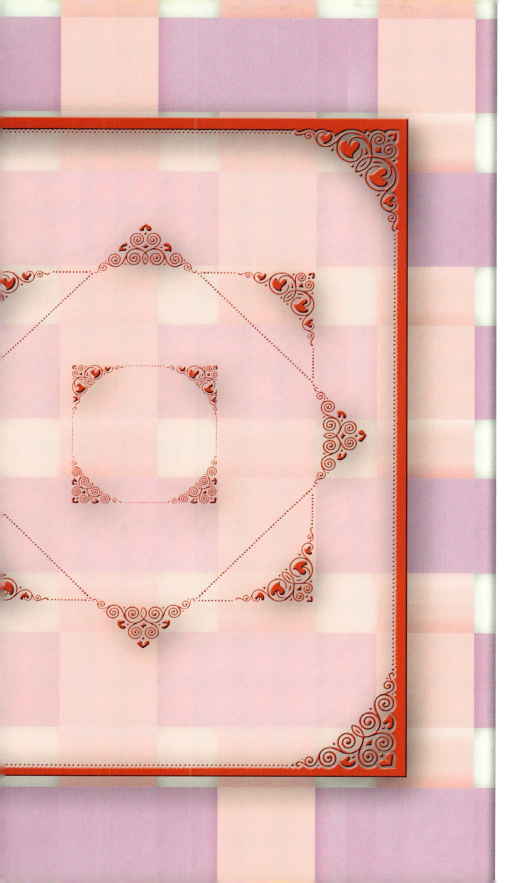

075

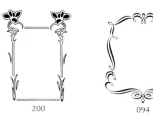

200  094

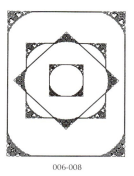

006-008

BT 036

**Techniques Used:**
Fill, Gradient, Clipping Mask, Scale, Rotate, Bevel/Emboss

| | | | | |
|---|---|---|---|---|
| | 0c | 38m | 100y | 2k |
| | 0c | 99m | 85y | 0k |
| | 10c | 30m | 0y | 0k |
| | 0c | 23m | 5y | 0k |
| | 245r | 166g | 24b | |
| | 238r | 32g | 53b | |
| | 222r | 185g | 216b | |
| | 250r | 206g | 215b | |

GALLERY

106

098

BT 011    BT 025    BT 034

**Techniques Used:**
Fill, Gradient, Drop Shadow, Clipping Mask, Scale, Rotate, Bevel/Emboss

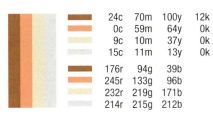

| 24c | 70m | 100y | 12k |
| 0c | 59m | 64y | 0k |
| 9c | 10m | 37y | 0k |
| 15c | 11m | 13y | 0k |
| 176r | 94g | 39b | |
| 245r | 133g | 96b | |
| 232r | 219g | 171b | |
| 214r | 215g | 212b | |

25

## About These Tutorials

The following are basic instructional tutorials for the techniques used to create the illustrations within the Gallery section of this book. These illustrations were created using Adobe Illustrator, and a basic working knowledge of this program is important to mastering these techniques. More in-depth information about this program can be found under the Adobe Illustrator Help tab, or by visiting the Adobe website at www.adobe.com.

These tutorials have been performed using the Macintosh version of Adobe Illustrator CS2. If you have a newer or older version of Illustrator, some variation could occur in how your software displays the tools used in these tutorials. Also, there are minor differences in functionality and nomenclature between the Windows and Macintosh versions of Illustrator. Consult your Illustrator manual or the Help tab if you do not find the Tool, Window, Menu, or Palette described in the tutorial.

## Opening Vectors in Illustrator

1. On the top menu bar, go to the drop-down menu File>Open.
2. In the Open window, locate the Dover CD which is in your computer's CD drive, double click.
3. Double click on the "Images" folder
4. Double click on the subfolder that contains the image that you wish to open.
5. Double click on the vector file that you wish to open.

## Some Basics about Vectors

Unlike bit-mapped images which are composed of pixels, vector graphics use points, lines, and curves to define shapes. Because of this they are "resolution independent," and can be reshaped, scaled, or resized without a loss of image quality. Please note that the final quality of your image will be determined by the resolution of your printer, or when viewing on-screen, by the quality of your monitor.

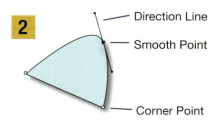

1. A vector "path" can either be open (like the curved line) or closed (like the circle).

2. Paths are made up of segments that create the entire shape. Each segment is defined by anchor points. Anchor points can be corner points or smooth points; points can be manipulated using direction lines to change the curvature of the segment.

# The Tool Bar and Palettes in Illustrator

**TUTORIALS**

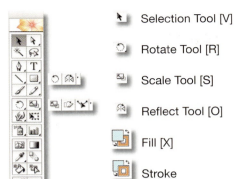

- Selection Tool [V]
- Rotate Tool [R]
- Scale Tool [S]
- Reflect Tool [O]
- Fill [X]
- Stroke

This is a list of the basic tools used in the tutorials. If the Tool bar is not displayed it can be accessed from the top menu bar by going to Window>Tools. The Tool bar is extremely handy, and gives quick access to the basic design tools. Some variant tools are hidden from view, and can be accessed by clicking and holding down the mouse over a related tool's icon. Tools with variants have small arrows in the bottom right hand corner of their icon.

To learn more about the Tool bar, search under the Help tab, or in the manual that accompanied your software.

This is a list of the basic Palettes used in the tutorials. Most palettes can be accessed from the top menu bar by going to Window>Palettes.
Please note that in Adobe Illustrator Palettes can also be referred to as Windows.

Swatches Palette    Layers Palette    Gradient Palette    Transform Palette    Align Palette

# Vector Software Resources

In addition to Adobe Illustrator and Photoshop, for which we have included instructional material within this book, there are many other software programs that allow you to use and edit vector-based images. Most of these programs are proprietary and must be purchased, however, there are several open-source, freeware and shareware programs available for download over the Internet. A good resource for information about both commercial and free software can be found at the following link:

http://en.wikipedia.org/wiki/List_of_vector_graphics_editors

There are several basic types of software programs with which vector images can be utilized.
The following is a list of the most popular, by category.

**Illustration**:

Adobe Illustrator    www.adobe.com/products/illustrator
Corel Draw    www.corel.com
Microsoft Expression Suite    www.microsoft.com/expression

**Page layout:**

Adobe InDesign    www.adobe.com/products/indesign
Quark XPress    www.quark.com
Scribus    www.scribus.net

**Web and web animation:**

Adobe Flash    www.adobe.com/products/flash
Adobe Fireworks    www.adobe.com/products/fireworks

**Photo editing:**

Adobe Photoshop    www.adobe.com/products/photoshop
Paint Shop Pro    www.corel.com

**Image editors:**

Xara Xtreme    www.xara.com
Inkscape    www.inkscape.org

## About Dover Vectors

Most of the vector images contained in this book come from rare, old sources. In creating these vectors we have tried to maintain the unique intrinsic qualities of the original artwork, while imbuing them with all of the utility that the vector file format affords. Generally, the images in this publication are of two types: regular, closed-cell illustrations which can be "released" into individual, manipulable shapes; and more expressive, "hand-drawn" illustrations. Please note that because of the complex nature of the latter, the best results in working with this type of image require a fast computer with large allocation of RAM. The simplest method for making more RAM available to Adobe Illustrator is to shut down all unnecessary software programs.

The expressive potential of compositions made with vector images is limitless. In addition to print layouts they can be used to create silkscreen stencils, embroidery patterns, or signage designs to be cut in vinyl. They can be combined with bit-mapped images, used as paths along which type can be flowed, or as texture in multilayered compositions. Vectors tend to be relatively small files, and work very well with programs that generate web graphics, such as Adobe Flash and Fireworks. We encourage you to experiment with these images and to be creative!

## Scaling an Image in Illustrator

**1** 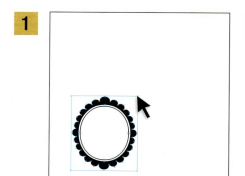  **2** 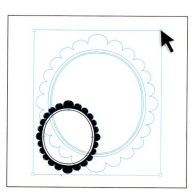  **3**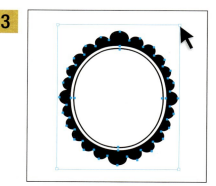

**4**

1. Select the image using the Selection Tool found at the top left corner of the tool bar [V]. A box will appear around the image.
2. Grab one of the corners of the box and drag it out diagonally to enlarge it. To reduce the image, drag it in. To scale the image proportionally, hold down the shift key while dragging.

**5**

3. Enlarged image.

4. You can also enlarge the image with the Transform Palette. Click the chain icon at the right of the palette to link the width and height together and scale proportionally.
5. To scale proportionally, enter either the desired width or height. To scale non-proportionally, both width and height must be entered.
6. Try the Scale Tool [S] found in the tool bar to achieve similar results.

# Flipping Images in Illustrator

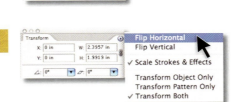

**This is also called reflecting the image.**

1. Select the image using the Selection Tool found at the top left corner of the tool bar [V].
2. On the top menu bar, go to the drop-down menu Window>Transform to open the Transform Palette. Click on the arrow in the upper right hand corner of the palette.
3. Choose Flip Horizontal
4. The image should be a mirror "reflection" of the original image.
5. This process can also be achieved using the Reflect Tool [O] found in the tool bar.

# Rotating an Image in Illustrator

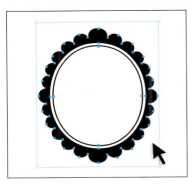
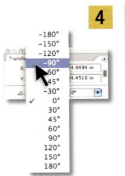
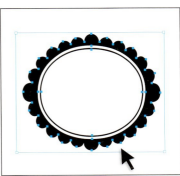

1. Select the image using the Selection Tool found at the top left corner of the tool bar [V].
2. On the top menu bar, go to the drop-down menu Window>Transform to open the Transform Palette. Click on the arrow next to the rotate input field at the lower left of the palette.
3. Select the desired angle from the pop-up list or enter the desired angle directly into the field.
4. The image should rotate.
5. The Rotate Tool [R] found in the tool bar can produce similar results.

# Adding Color to Your Palette in Illustrator

**At some point you will want to add colors to your palette. Here is one way to do this.**

1. On the top menu bar, go to the drop-down menu Windows>Swatches. This will open the Swatches Palette window. Select a color swatch. Click the Add New Swatch button in the lower right corner of the window next to the trashcan.
2. The Swatch Options window should appear. Change the color using the sliders at the bottom of the palette. You can change the mode using the drop-down Color Mode button. The global option will allow you to assign a color and change it globally in your document. Color type can be either Spot for PMS spot colors or Process for CMYK process colors.
3. When you finish creating the color swatch, type in a name for it and click the OK button.
4. Figure 4 shows the new orange swatch in the palette.
5. To add additional colors, repeat steps 1, 2, and 3.

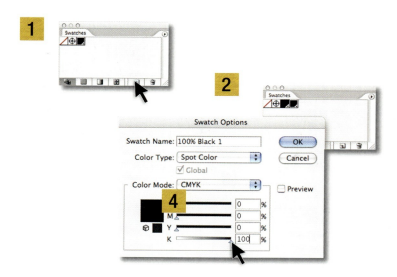

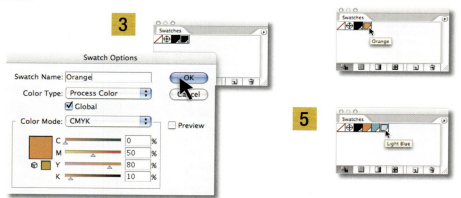

# Using a Limited Palette

A limited color palette helps you organize, harmonize, and set the mood for individual projects. A cool palette might consist of blues and grays; while a warmer palette would have more reds and yellows. If you are designing an image of a sunset, you won't need cool colors, so why add them to your palette?

Most of the examples shown in this book give the color palette used for both CMYK and RGB color modes.

## Fills in Illustrator

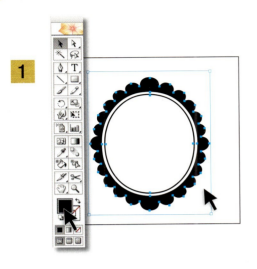
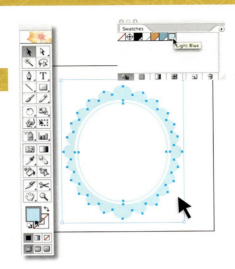

1. Select the image using the Selection Tool found at the top left corner of the tool bar [V].

   Select the fill square from the tool bar [K].

2. Fill the image by clicking on a color from the Swatches Palette window.

**TUTORIALS**

## Strokes or Outlines in Illustrator

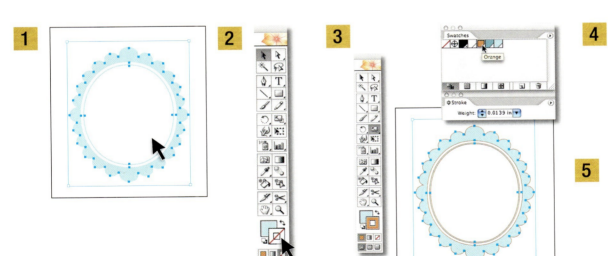
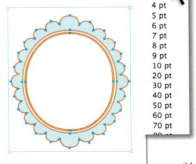

1. Select the image using the Selection Tool found at the top left corner of the tool bar [V].
2. Select the stroke square from the tool bar [X].
3. Stroke the image by clicking on a color from the Swatches Palette window.
4. Change the size of the stroke by clicking on the blue arrow to the immediate right of the stroke input field.
5. Choose the designed stroke weight from the pop-up window or type in the desired weight.

31

# Releasing a Compound Path in Illustrator

1
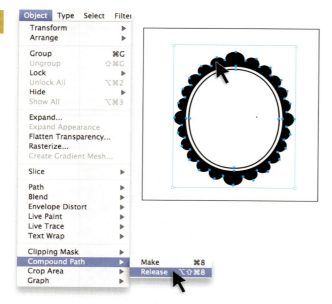

2
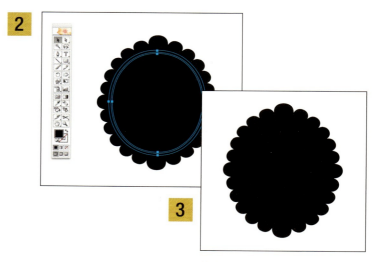

3

**In order to work (color, stroke, drop shadow, etc.) with the individual cells in a compound path, you need to release the compound path.**

1. Select the image using the Selection Tool found at the top left corner of the tool bar [V].

   Go to the drop-down menu Object>Compound Path>Release on the top menu bar.

2. Your image should look similar to Figure 2. Each individual shape that comprises the image is highlighted.

   These shapes are now independent of each other.

3. Deselect the image.

4. Select the image again and fill the top shape with a color.

5. With the shape still selected go to the drop-down menu Object>Arrange>Send to Back on the top menu bar.

4
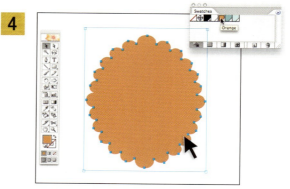

5
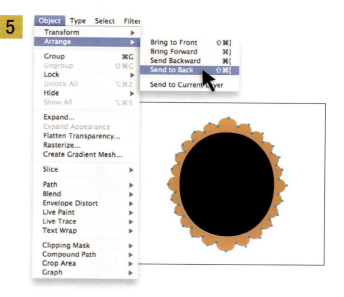

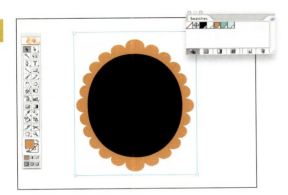

6. The colored shape should now be behind all the other shapes.

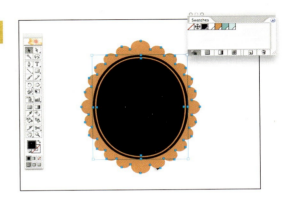

7. Select one of the black shapes remaining and fill with a color.

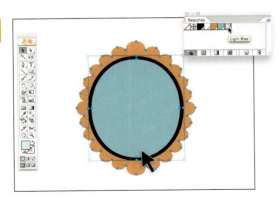

8. Once a new color has been applied to the shape, your image should look similar to Figure 8.

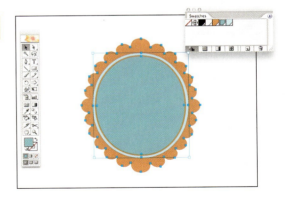

9. Continue selecting the shapes and filling them with color to complete the image.

# Working with Layers in Illustrator

**1**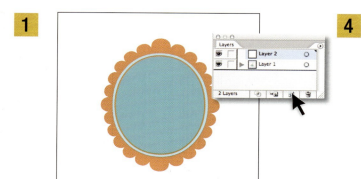

**2**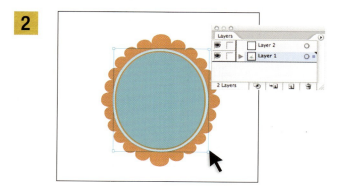

**3**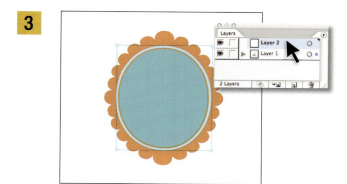

**4**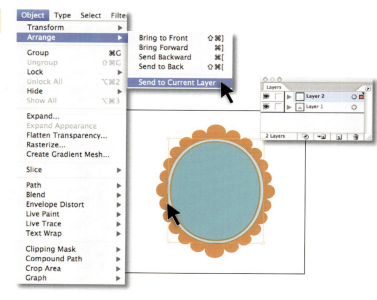

1. On the top menu bar, go to the drop-down menu Window>Layers to open the Layers window. Create a new layer by clicking the New Layer button located in the lower right corner next to the trashcan.

2. Select the images or shapes you want to move to a new layer using the Selection Tool found at the top left corner of the tool bar [V].

3. With the images still highlighted, reselect the new layer (layer 2) by clicking the radio button next to the layer name.

4. On the top menu bar go to the drop-down menu Object>Arrange>Send to Current Layer. This will send all the shapes selected in step 2 to layer 2.

# Gradients in Illustrator

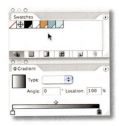

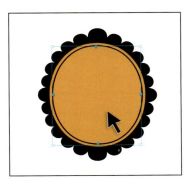
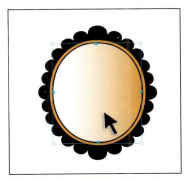

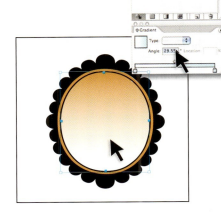

1. On the top menu bar, go to the drop-down menu Window>Swatches and Window>Gradient. This will open the Swatches and Gradient Palette windows.

2. Select the color you want to make into a gradient from the Swatches Palette and hold the left mouse button down while dragging the color swatch to the Gradient Palette window.

3. The swatch is placed on either the left or right hand swatch boxes on the gradient slider. The basic gradient should look similar to Figure 3. You can adjust the gradient by moving the sliders and by dragging additional color swatches to the Gradient Palette window.

4. In the upper left hand corner of the Gradient Palette window will be the gradient you have just created. Select it and hold the left mouse button down while dragging it to the Swatches Palette.

   Note: The All Swatches button at the bottom of the Swatches Palette must be clicked in order to see regular colors together with gradients.

5. Your Swatch Palette should look similar to Figure 5.

6. Select the image you want to apply your new gradient to using the Selection Tool found at the top left corner of the tool bar [V].

7. Select your new gradient from the Swatches Palette. Your image should look similar to Figure 7.

8. To change the angle of a gradient, select the object containing the gradient, then type in a new angle in the angle input field in the Gradient Palette window.

# Clipping Masks in Illustrator

**Using a Clipping Mask to Fill a Vector Shape with a Bitmap Image**

1. On the top menu bar, go to the drop-down menu File>Place. Select the bitmap image you want to place using the Place Dialog Box, then click the place button. The bitmap image will be on the art board, but will be in front of the vector shape.

2. If it is not already highlighted, select the bitmap image using the Selection Tool found at the top left corner of the tool bar [V]. On the top menu bar, go to the drop-down menu Object>Arrange> Send to Back. This will move the bitmap image behind the vector shape.

3. While holding down the shift key, select both the bitmap image and vector shape using the Selection Tool found at the top left corner of the tool bar [V]. On the top menu bar, go to the drop-down menu Object>Clipping Mask>Make.

4. The bitmap image will fill the vector shape.

# Opening EPS Vector Images in Photoshop

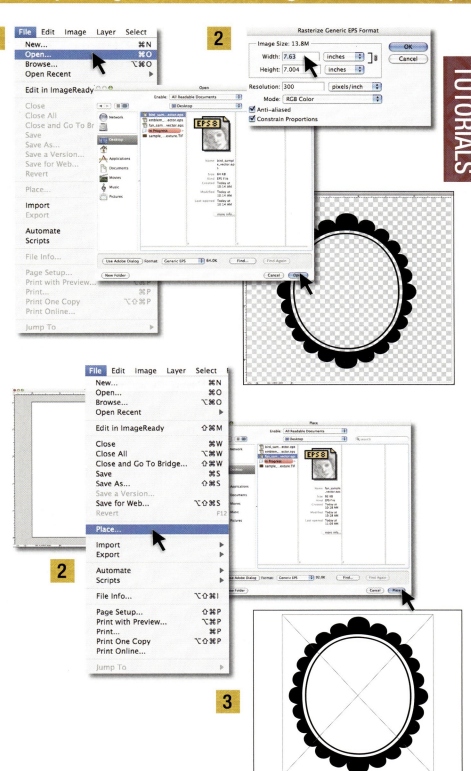

## Opening a EPS Vector in Photoshop

1. On the top menu bar, go to the drop-down menu File>Open. In the Open Window, find and select the EPS Vector file you want to open and click the Open button.

2. In the Rasterize Generic EPS Format Window, be sure to select a size that is large enough to fill your document. Because you are rasterizing the EPS, you will not be able to scale the image again without losing quality.

   Remember when working with pixel-based formats in Photoshop, it is always easier to scale down than up. Only EPS Vector files allow you to scale your images without loss of quality before embedding them into your Photoshop document. Not all EPS files are true vector-based objects.

## Placing a EPS Vector in Photoshop

1. Be sure to have a blank or working document already open.

2. On the top menu bar, go to the drop-down menu File>Place. In the Open Window, find and select the EPS Vector file you want to place and click the Place button.

3. The EPS Vector will be placed in your blank document and will retain many of its vector-based qualities until it is rasterized. In Photoshop, this is called a Smart Object, since you can still edit it in its native format with a program such as Adobe Illustrator. Read more about Smart Objects in your Photoshop Web Help or the manual that accompanied your software.

## Selecting Areas with the Magic Wand in Photoshop

**1**

**2**

**3**

1. Select the Magic Wand Tool [W] found in the tool bar.
2. Enter a value in the Tolerance field found near the top menu bar. The higher this value, the wider the range of colors that will be selected. You can change this value in accordance to the type of image you are using.
3. Select an area of the image.

## Adding Color with the Paint Bucket in Photoshop

**1**  **2**

1. Select the Paint Bucket Tool [G] found in the tool bar.

   The Paint Bucket will use the color assigned to the foreground color box

2. Paint the object by clicking on it.

## Adding Color to a Selected Area in Photoshop

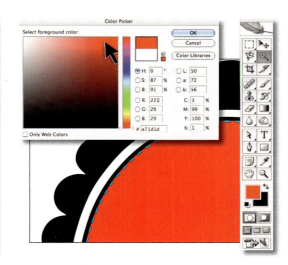

1. Select an area of the image using the Magic Wand Tool [W] found in the tool bar.
2. Double-click the Foreground Color box found at the bottom of the tool bar and open the Color Picker Palette. Select a color and click OK. The new color should display in the Foreground Color box in the tool bar.
3. On the top menu bar, go to the drop-down menu Edit>Fill. Select Foreground Color from the Fill Dialog Box and click OK
4. The section will be filled with the foreground color.

# Layering Images in Photoshop

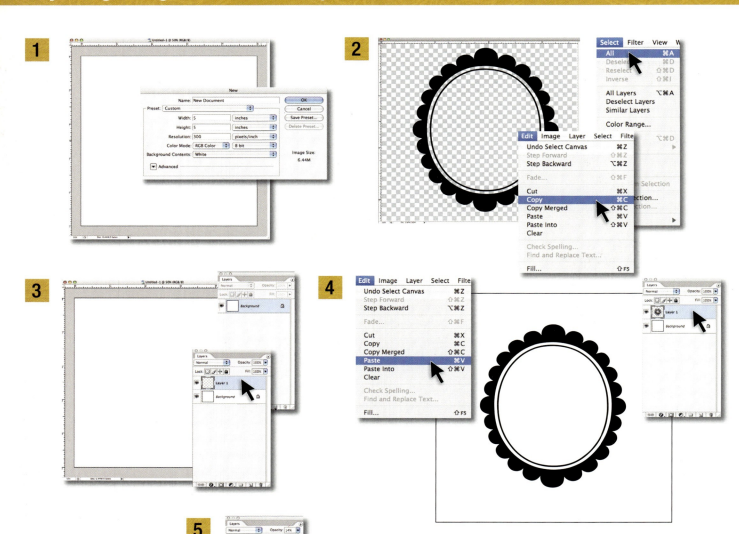

1. On the top menu bar, go to the drop-down menu File>New and create a new blank document.

2. On the top menu bar, go to the drop-down menu File>Open; find and select the EPS Vector file you want in your new document; click the Open button. On the top menu bar, go to the drop-down menu Select>All, then go to the drop-down menu Edit>Copy.

3. Go to the Layers window in the new blank document made in step 1, and create a new layer by clicking on the New Layer button at the lower right corner next to the trash can.

4. On the top menu bar, go to the drop-down menu Edit>Paste. The vector shape copied in step 2 should now be on Layer 2. Repeat Steps 3 and 4 to add additional layers and images.

5. To change the opacity of a layer, select the layer; click the arrow to the right of the Opacity field, and use the slider to manipulate the opacity.

# Adding a Gradient with Photoshop Layer Styles

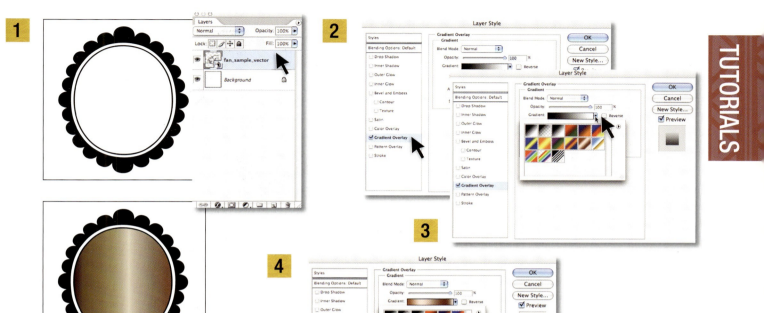

1. In the Layers window, double-click the layer you want to add a style to. This will open the Layer Style window.
2. In this window, select Gradient Overlay in the list of styles at the left of the window to open the Gradient Options window.
3. Click the arrow at the right end of the gradient sample bar.
4. Choose a gradient from the pop-up menu.
5. Click the gradient swatch to open the Gradient Editor window. Click on any of the color stop boxes to choose new colors.
6. In the Color Picker window, select a new color and click OK.

   You can also change the position of the color stop boxes by sliding them along the gradient bar.

# Adding Texture to Line Art in Photoshop

1. Open a line art EPS image from the CD. (see page 37) Then convert its color space to RBG by going to the top menu bar, drop-down menu Image>Mode>RGB.

2. Open a background texture image from the CD.

3. Select a cell of the image using the Magic Wand Tool [W] found in the tool bar. (see page 38)

   Be sure to set the tolerance at 32, with both Anti-Alias and Contiguous checked when making your selection.

   Smooth the selection 2 pixels via the top menu bar, drop-down menu Select>Modify>Smooth. Click OK.

   Then expand the selection by 2 pixels by going to the top menu bar, drop-down menu Select>Modify>Expand. Click OK.

4. Click on the texture document you want to incorporate into the selected cell.

   On the top menu bar, go to the drop-down menu Select>All. This should select the entire image.

   Then from the top menu bar, go to the drop-down menuEdit>Copy. This will copy the selection.

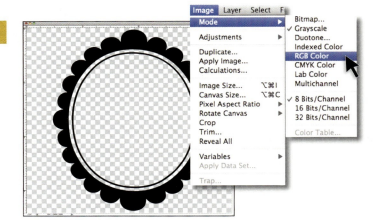

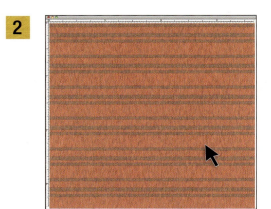

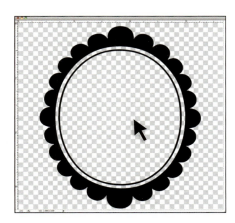

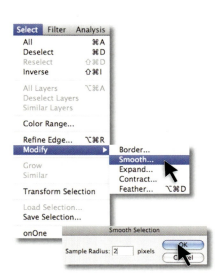

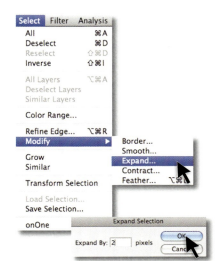

4

5

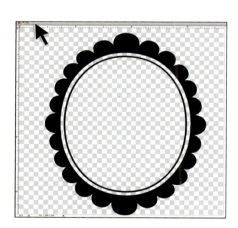 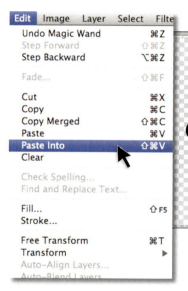 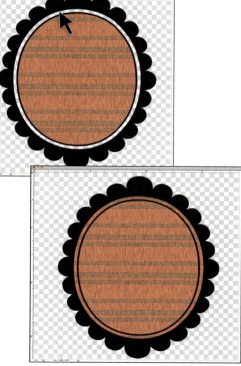

5. Click back on the line art image. Be sure a cell is still selected, if not repeat step 3.

   On the top menu bar, go to the drop-down menu Edit>Paste Into. The copy (step 4) of the texture image should be pasted inside the selected cell.

   Repeat Steps 2 thru 5 to finish filling in the cells.

TUTORIALS

**1**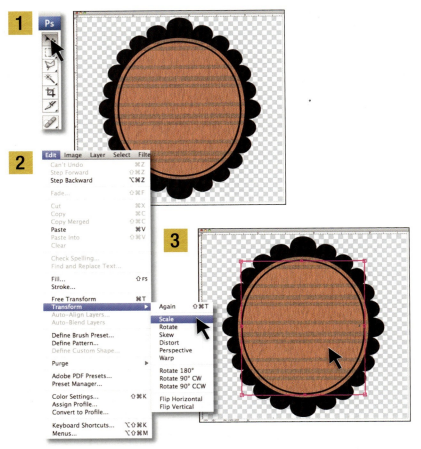

Once the texture images have been pasted into the line art (see pages 42-43), they can then be transformed to achieve more realistic effects.

1. To scale the texture, select an individual layer with the Selection Tool [V] found at the top of the Tool Bar. This should also highlight the Layer the texture is on as well.

2. On the top menu bar, go to the drop-down menu Edit>Transform>Scale.

3. Scale the image using the handles that pop-up around the selection.

   When the image has been scaled to your liking simply double click the left mouse button and the transform will be set.

4. To rotate the texture select an individual layer with the Selection Tool [V] found at the top of the Tool Bar.

5. On the top menu bar, go to the drop-down menu Edit>Transform>Rotate.

6. Rotate the image using the handles that pop-up around the selection.

   When the image has been rotated to your liking simply double click the left mouse button and the transform will be set.

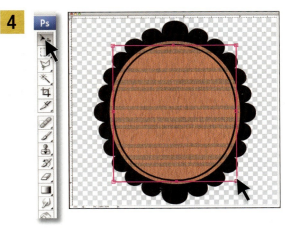

44

## Changing the Hue of the Texture in Photoshop

The expressive range of the 40 texture samples supplied on the CD can be dramatically expanded by using the Hue and Saturation function in Photoshop.

**TUTORIALS**

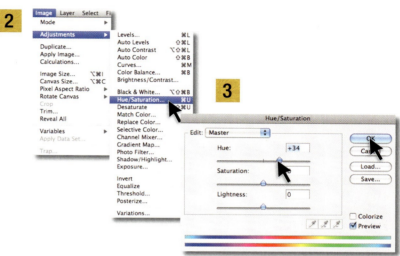

1. To change the color of the textures select an individual layer with the Selection Tool [V] found at the top of the Tool Bar.
2. On the top menu bar, go to the drop-down menu Image>Adjustments>Hue/Saturation.
3. In the Hue/Saturation dialog box simply vary the color using the Hue Slider Bar.

   Once you have the color that you want click the OK button to set the new color.

   Continue this process to create a visually stunning piece of digital art.

003

004

VECTORS

49

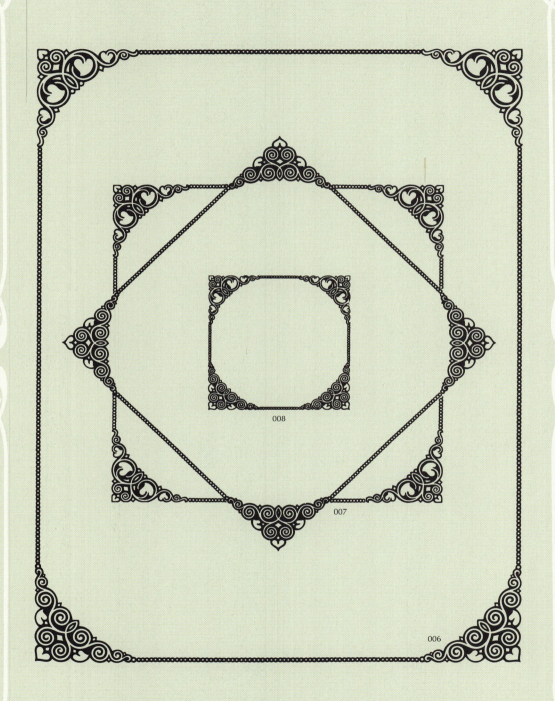

025

026

027

028

56

030

029

VECTORS

074

073

072

071

075
076

089
090

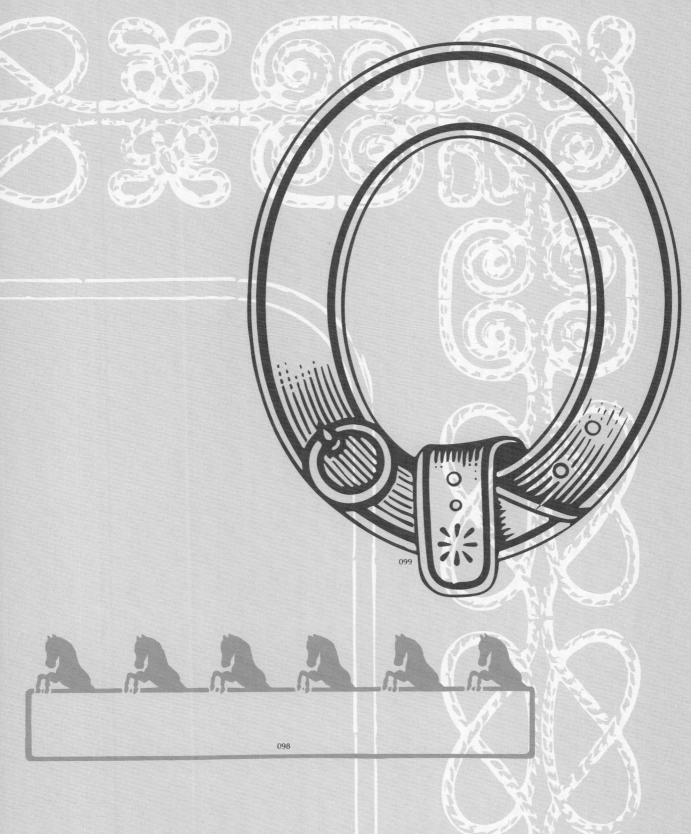

VECTORS

102

103

87

122
123

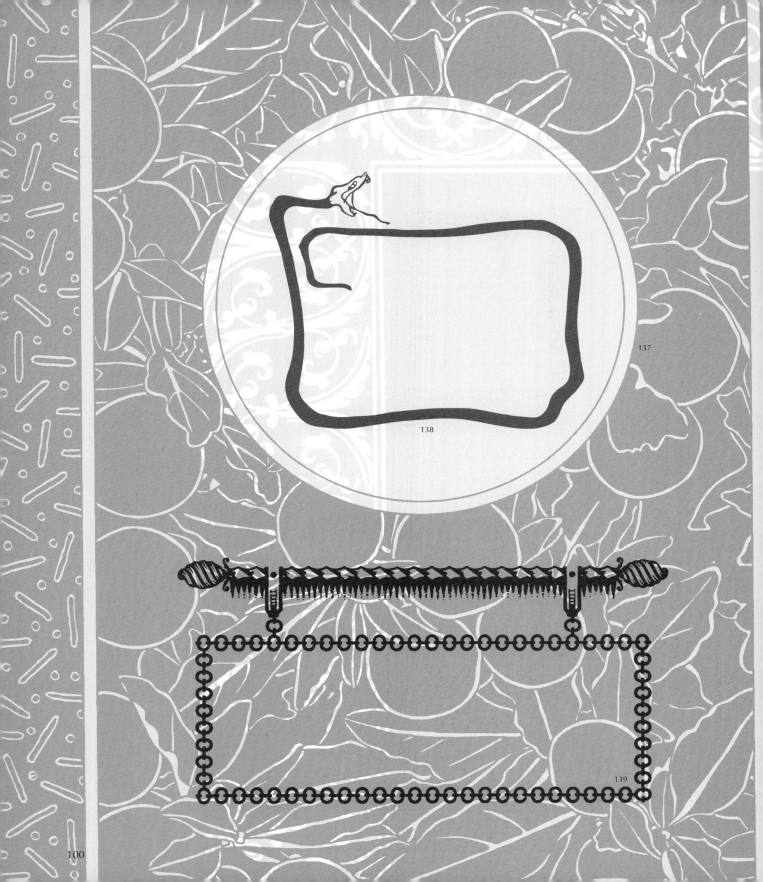

145

144

160
161

163

165
164

169
170

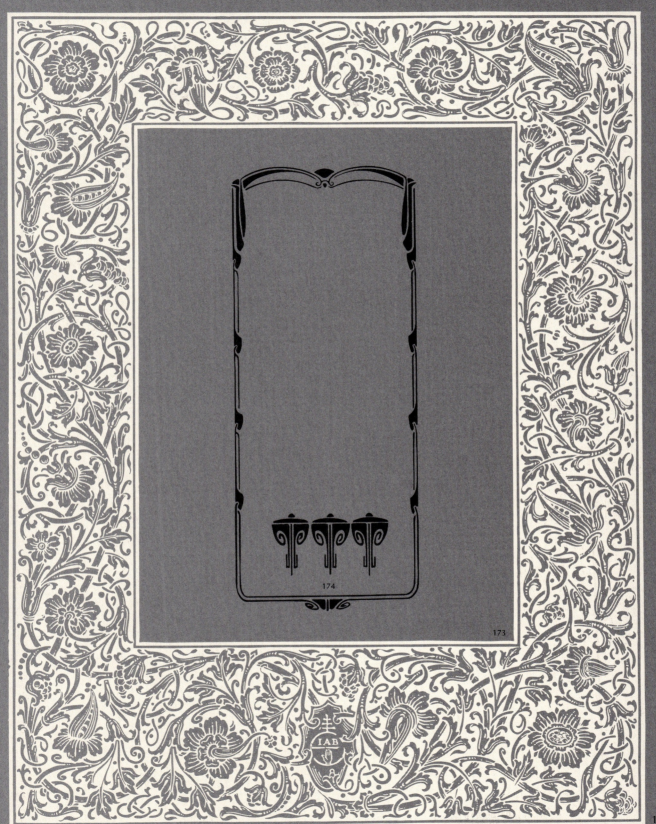

# VECTORS

SARAH

ISAAC

ABRAHAM

LEOPOLD

187
188

197

198

203-206

## WHAT'S ON THE CD

EPS and SVG vector files of all of the images in the Vectors section.
JPG bit-mapped files of all of the images in the Vectors section.
JPG files of all of the bitmap textures used in the Gallery section.
JPG files of all of the illustrations in the Gallery section of the book.
Dover Design Manager

## SOFTWARE AND HARDWARE REQUIREMENTS

The vector images on the included CD are suitable for use on computers running Windows 98, 2000, XP, Vista, and Windows 7; or Macintosh OS 9.1–OS X. The computer should have sufficient RAM to power the type of graphics software program with which these image files are intended for use; 256MB minimum, 512MB recommended.

To fully utilize these vector images they must be used with an illustration program such as Adobe Illustrator®, Macromedia Freehand®, or Corel Draw®, or a web animation program such as Adobe Flash®. The images can also be opened, but with limited functionality, in pixel image-editing programs such as Adobe Photoshop®, Adobe Photoshop Elements®, and Corel PaintShop®. This book and CD does not contain any of the above software.

The vector images in this book were based on artwork taken from the following previously published Dover titles:

*372 Frames and Borders CD-ROM and Book,* by Dover
*Dover Digital Design Source #1: Victorian Frames and Borders,* by Dover
*Old-Fashioned Frames,* by Dover
*Art Nouveau Frames and Borders,* by Dover
*Decorative Frames and Borders,* by Edmund V. Gillon, Jr.
*Art Nouveau Decorative Borders and Frames,* by Carol Belanger Grafton
*Borders and Frames,* by Dover
*Banners, Ribbons and Scrolls,* by Dover
*Ready-to-Use Old-Fashioned Floral Borders on Layout Grids,* by Carol Belanger Grafton
*Treasury of Authentic Art Nouveau: Alphabets, Decorative Initials, Monograms, Frames and Ornaments,* by Ludwig Petzendorfer
*Ready-To-Use Art Deco Borders,* by Ted Menten
*Borders, Frames and Decorations of the Art Nouveau Period,* by Carol Belanger Grafton
*New Art Deco Borders and Motifs,* by William Rowe
*Decorative Wreaths and Frames CD-ROM and Book,* by Dover